COHERENCE

DR. MANNAT ATWAL

ZORBA BOOKS

A collection of 15 poems that will take you on a rollercoaster of emotions. Apart from the themes of love, pain, courage and failure, this one encapsulates vulnerabilities, which is quite difficult to explore. The word play is intriguing and will make you ponder.

The poignant writing style will make you feel the deceit and hurt which the poet has tried to convey. It will leave you a little heavy-hearted. But in the end, you will find that ray of hope to survive through your struggles.

Anybody who has ever felt pain in love will resonate deeply with the poems. Each poem is not too short, with enough fodder to pack a punch.

From moving on from the past, pure love, being forlorn, overcoming demons to the musings of a bleeding heart, the reader will experience the bleeding pen on paper.

Definitely recommend!
- Anushree Saha @mywordbubble

ZORBA BOOKS

Published by Zorba Books, December 2023
Website: www.zorbabooks.com
Email: info@zorbabooks.com

Title: **Coherence**

Author Name: Dr. Mannat Atwal

Printbook ISBN :- 978-93-5896-998-6

Ebook ISBN :- 978-93-5896-432-5

Zorba Books Pvt. Ltd. (opc)
Sushant Arcade,
Next to Courtyard Marriot,
Sushant Lok 1, Gurgaon – 122009, India

Printed in India

TO YOU,
A FEW CHAPTERS LATER

PREFACE

In the quiet corners of the human heart, there exists a realm where shadows dance, and emotions, both beautiful and haunting, intertwine. It is in this ethereal space that the verses within these pages come to life. Since time immemorial, I believed that there is a certain side to the dark emotional fiend within us which only some of us can comprehend. While I was crafting these pages, I frequently penned down observations of the emotional journeys that people in my surroundings underwent. At a personal level, I found it tough to resonate with these mere emotions and tried to give them a shape in the form of words. Each sonnet in this collection is a testament to the power of language to capture the essence of our deepest fears, sorrows, and desires. Verses that embrace melancholy, despair, and an acknowledgement that darkness is not devoid of its own allure, and within its depths, we often uncover our most authentic selves.

ACKNOWLEDGEMENT

To bring this collection of dark poetry to life, I owe my deepest gratitude to those who have illuminated my path and inspired the verses within these pages.

I take this opportunity to express my heartfelt gratitude towards my family, whose unwavering support and encouragement have been my anchor throughout this creative journey. Your belief in me has been a constant source of strength.

To my friends, whose conversations and shared experiences have shaped my understanding of the human soul. Thank you for being both muses and companions on this poetic expedition.

Finally, yet significantly, I wish to express my gratitude to a character who served as my inspiration, a wellspring of my creative energy, and the driving force behind my determination- Eren Jäeger. Without analyzing Eren's traits, I would never have embarked on the path of composing this book or conquering the depths of my own inner fiend. To the reader who now holds this book in their hands, your willingness to embark on this poetic journey, to explore the dark corners of the

human heart and psyche, is the ultimate gift. It is you who gives meaning and purpose to these words.

Thank you for being a part of this literary voyage. May these poems resonate with your own emotions, and may they inspire you to embrace the beauty that exists even in the deepest shadows.

CONTENTS

POEM 1
MIND TO EYES

The sun shone through the curtains on you
Although I woke before you
Only to be laying in sleep, feeling blue.
I told you to stay shut
since our heart is feeling cut
But the morning rays beamed at you
Again no good coming today is something only I knew.

You drew away those eyelids like curtains
A pit in our heart, to you I ascertained.
Your lips tried to form a smiling curve
The sadness in you only I observed.

You saw yourself in the mirror
The pain in you became sheerer
You blinked
Blood inked;
Soreness around you
I tell you it'll be fine, although untrue.
You looked for a view;
Like they say 'a sight for sore eyes'
You search more and once again our heart dies.
Wrenched in disappointment yet again
Can our 'soft piece of wax' really be blamed?

Through the long day
You searched astray
I say 'Be brave'
Another path tomorrow may be paved
Where we find someone
In this long run.

The sun sets
You look down in regret
All those people that you left
You still accuse them of theft
Theft of trust
Theft of hope
Theft of love
Theft of scope.

Tears now leaving you
The ones you left may be grieving you
Is this why we feel blue?
Because we thought all of it was true?
A painting in me you drew
Of the ones, away from whom you flew
Yet their thoughts in me are glued.

Coherence

Dear eyes, I'm tired of you
Only seeing the good
No lessons it seems that you understood
If not for you, then do it for me
For the longest I've yearned for peace
Let me turn over this old leaf
No more can I welcome grief.
I wish to wake up tomorrow with some relief.
I say 'Be brave'
Another path tomorrow may be paved
Where we find someone
In this long run
Till then take care, just be numb.

POEM 2
A WHISPER FROM MY DEMONS

I did lend my ears
to my demons, to my fears
They told me to write about myself, all parts of me glued
glued together on a sheet
about the times on my pure heart, I decided to cheat.
Times I betrayed it for peace
For love
For deceit.
For gain,
Swallowed pain.
For desire,
Lit my soul on fire.

They told me to paint with words , a sonnet all blue
All colours that depict my pure soul's hue
Pure or impure I cannot decide
So you be the judge, while here I just write.
I write about my sins
My confessions
My broken wings.

For once I broke someone's soul
Their heart so pure
And then she would never show her eyes
Scared of the lies.
Now when I look at the night sky
I still feel her silent cry
I feel her ache
I feel her pain
The chaos in her brain
The teary eyes that are drained
The heart that loved in vain
And she isn't me, is what I'll claim.

Now in the end, the judge that is you
A small alteration if you'll allow me into
All that you read ,all about my hue
Let's reverse every word that seemed written true
For one thing I forgot to mention to you
The demons whispered to me, 'write a sonnet about you, in
which nothing is true'
For that's what they do
For that's their rule
To turn you from true to untrue
Till you allow them to rule you.
All about the hue
All that was written, untrue
Because that girl who weeps through and through
Is none other than me, yes it's true.

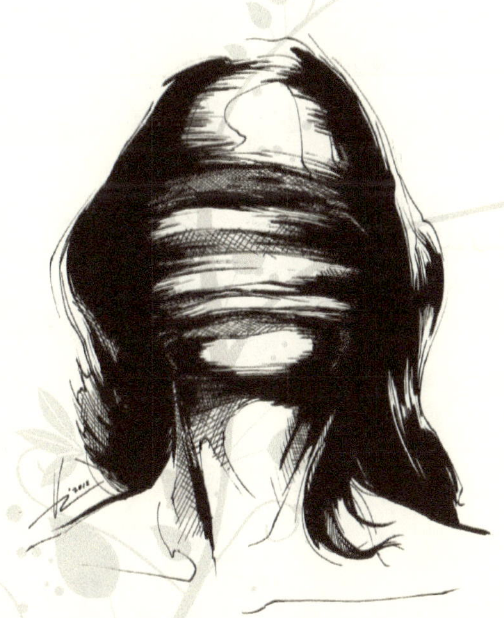

POEM 3
WEATHER OF MY MIND

It's been raining a lot lately
About my eyes I write this bravely.
The droplets of this rain don't seem to stop
Like a cloud has burst on top
In my stomach I still feel a knot
My heart feels like it's been shot.

The weather of my mind
These tears make me blind
The ones I loved, left me behind
Yet everyone expects me to be kind.

After the rain comes the sun
But for my eyes, they still feel numb
The tears washed away my grief
The light will find it through, I do believe.

My subconscious is like the clouds
In different emotions it forms about
Any emotion left in me? I doubt
Then how do I get rid of this heavy cloud?
It causes rain
After a while all the tears do drain
Yet my eyes are left feeling piercing pain.

The weather of my mind
Still makes me blind
To love
To hate
Then why not to pain?

But after the rain comes the sun
Even if my eyes do feel numb
The tears will wash away my grief
A light coming soon, I'll still believe.

POEM 4
YOUR ROLE

You could be an angel
They'll be disturbed by your wings
You could be the devil
They won't even have to say a thing
You could be as innocent
They'll pull you with their strings
You could be you
They'll find a way to paint you blue.

You could be the sunlight
They'll call it too bright
You could be the moonlight
They'll say you never shine
You could be a star
They'll say you think you're too high above
You could be you
Yet they'll find a way to drown you too.

Coherence

You could be so warm
They'll call you 'calm before the storm'
You could be so cold
They'll highlight you in bold
You could be the monsoon rain
They'll say your energy is too faint
You could be you
Yet they'll choose another above you.

You could guide them all the way
Yet they'll leave you astray
You could play mind games
They'll try to seize the day
You could be the best
They'll say you're different than the rest.

You should be you
Don't let them paint your hue
Whether kind
Emotionally blind
Whether blessed
Or emotionless.
Pick your poison; devil or angel
They'll anyway put a label
So pick your own card
Don't be the target to their dart
For one thing they'll never know
The devil was once an angel who chose not to fold.

POEM 5
FALL

Maple leaves fall to the ground
Just like that part of you, to which you were bound
A new season is yet to arrive
Time to part with that invisible knife
That carves through your windpipe
Now it's time to get on a new ride.
Because when Fall comes
Our tears do drain
When Fall comes
We shed our pain.

The season of mists and yellow tainted sky
Old parts of you are yet to die
Even the rain stops to welcome the Fall
Then why won't your tears stop to listen to your heart's call.
It's said that Nature is the most vibrant through Autumn,
Just like how you'll rise once you've hit rock bottom.

In this season, it's neither too warm nor cold
It's the perfect transition from calm to bold.
Now the old parts of you will be ready to burn
Whilst you'll be smiling in the autumn sun.
Away from those cuffs you cannot run
Just shed them off, it's the Fall season.

Maple leaves will fall to the ground
Heart wrenching memories will cloud around.
When you let go, to what you were bound
Everything in your heart, you will surmount.
Because when Fall comes,
Our tears do drain.
But when Fall comes,
We shed our pain.

POEM 6
UNDER
THIS POISONOUS TREE

I don't hurt
I don't ache
I don't trust
So there's no pain .

Do you understand me?
Below this poisonous tree
All that I've found is grief
Yet I try to turn over a new leaf

I read somewhere;
Grief is just love with nowhere to go
Truth be told, it got me feeling so low
And do I dare
To ever love again
To choose my heart over my brain?
To choose a path that may lead to pain?
No
I'd still choose to be low
And live with this love that has nowhere to go.

You ask me why I frown?
In the overwhelming pool of love should I drown?
And do I dare
Ever again
To Go back into that emotional affair,
the stars that night will look down,
Gaze at me and laugh about
They'll say that girl who was a fool
Cried a river, cried a brook
Some lessons it seems that she understood
But we know not why she swims back to that same old pool?

I read somewhere;
Grief is just love with nowhere to go
In that same brook will I never again flow.
Even though deep in my heart I feel a pit grow
That longs for love
That longs for care
But do I dare
To love again
All I'll ever know is immense pain.

Sometimes I do want to feel
An ounce of happiness, even if it's unreal
I think I've taken enough time to heal
And now I might be ready to make another one of Cupid's deal
My heart that now is made of steel
Before an ounce of love it may be forced to kneel.
Maybe I'll dare to care again
Maybe I'll choose some love over piercing pain
Maybe I'll go with the flow
And if in the end I'm left feeling low
I'll still live with this love that has nowhere to go.

POEM 7
TAP INTO DARKNESS

The darkness in you,
Turns everything vivid blue.
The moment one plus one makes two,
You toss them away like a tool.
You act like you're hurt
Till you rip away their gut.

You play and play
Lead their mind astray.
Mentor of their mind,
To your strings they bind
You pull them from behind
Yet somehow they establish you are kind.

The darkness in you
Turns everything vivid blue
It pulls them towards you
Till you want to keep them as a tool.
Like your own game of chess
Although your mind is a mess
Yet you shake away that distress
Your next move none could guess.

You keep your intentions concealed
Because you're dominated by your inner fiend.
The damage you cause cannot be unseen
Yet you keep your own hands clean.

There's more to this sonnet, if you may
More about you how play as night turns to day
I'd write more about you , all true
But that isn't something you'll allow me into.

Although secrets concealed
Yet one thing I'll reveal,
I know where you reside
Where you play and then hide
The one who writes this, it's you
Within me, yes it's true.

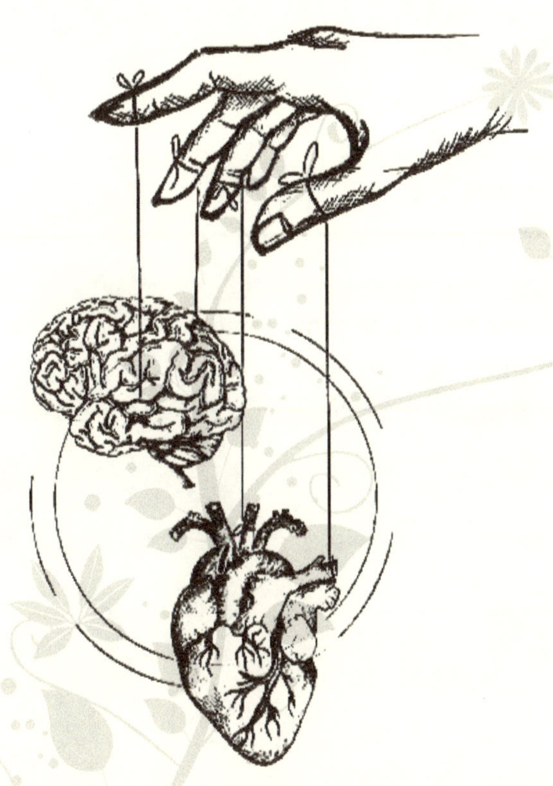

POEM 8
BOON OR BANE

I say it's for the best
But have I ruined myself?
I watch people hurt
Like how I used to ache
I watch people cry
Like how my eyes used to drain.

Life offers a deal of ups and downs
Though some we surmount
In some we choose to drown.

We say it's life
move ahead with a new drive.
It is what it is
It's not as it was
Then when through this entire cycle did our feelings take a pause?

We say let's move on
We say it's going to pass
And then comes the dawn
Where our heart's feeling torn.

We say it's in the past
We say let's move on
This too shall surpass
But let's hope this is the last.
Because through all these cycles, we go on and on
We let it pass, we do move on.
Although we say it's for the best
But in this process
Did we ruin ourselves?

POEM 9
BLEEDING HEART

I gave you my all
When in your eyes I chose to fall
Every bit of me was yours
Every part of me was pure

I gave you my hand
With you I chose to stand
Any moment without you seemed bland
We'd be together soon, I'd make myself understand
But upon giving you my hand
yours slipped out of mine
Just like the grains of sand
And Today all alone I stand.

I gave you a brush
Told you there was no rush
I was your canvas to paint
Have no restraint
Paint me how you like
I'll be yours with all my might
Just like the blue of the sky
You painted me yours with a smile
But soon your colour ran dry
And the blue of the day turned to night
And I was painted black in no time.
Yet again I tried to sparkle through that black sight
Just like the glittery sky from a starry night
But you chose to look away
And walked into the next day
And reminiscing about that starry sky, here in my bed I still lay.

I gave you my mind
I let you string it how you liked
Your thoughts would hit me in waves
Sometimes like a tornado in the bay
Still I chose to let you stay
Cuz if from this ocean of thoughts I tried to swim away,
In a deeper sea of longing, was I going to lay.
Yet I gave you my mind
Tossed in the sea of emotions
You drowned me through all your commotion.

And finally I gave you my heart
Thought we would never fall apart
Yet your words hit me like a dart
A dart on the target
You left me before our journey even started
Those days for me were the darkest
Back then I know I wasn't the smartest
Cuz' yet again I gave you my all for a new fresh start,
Thought we'd never fall apart
But then our ways did part
And today I sit and write this with a bleeding heart.

POEM 10
TILL I SEE YOU AGAIN

There will be days when it rains
Nights when there's pain
Mornings when you're drained
You may even lose your restraint
On those days don't stoop or strain.
Just keep moving forward
Till we unite again.

There will be times that you'll dread
Days when you won't have butter for your bread
Your patience may be as thin as a thread
On those days, remember not to lose your head
Just keep moving forward
Till we unite again.

You've flown far away
To a place that watches stars while here it's day
Maybe a little longer you were meant to stay
Yet not much will I say
Because we'll talk about it soon
When we unite again.

Dear me, who is reading this
Who overcame her demons and found some bliss
Who has a heart so full, yet emotionless
Who cherishes her inner demons, yet feels blessed.

Away from that naïve soul, you parted ways
You battled with yourself, as nights turned to days.
If this is how you chose to go on
Then this is the person into which now you have Sworn,
After killing that naïve soul, you seemed reborn
The rest of your story will hence be redrawn.
Because your soul has flown far away
To a place that watches stars while here it's day
Maybe a little longer she was meant to stay.
Yet not much will I say
Because we'll talk about it soon
When our sins unite again.

POEM 11
BARTER

To risk your heart, for love
To risk your mind, for tranquility
To risk loss, for a win
To risk war, for peace
To risk it all, knowing we could fall.

To protect love, we build hate
To protect peace, we fight
To protect the future, we change our fate
To protect ourselves, we test our might
To protect our needs, we sow more seeds
To protect it all, knowing our heart could bleed.

Those who do not risk, will never fall
Those who do not risk will never have it all
Those who do not risk, will never dream
Those who do not risk, their fate will sleep
To not risk at all, in their needs will crawl.

To place your heart on a platter
Knowing it could get cut
To place your peace on a sword
Just following your gut
To place your eyes on the prize
Knowing you could miss
To place your mind in a struggle
And trade away your bliss.

Those who do not know pain
Will never know peace
Those who do not know failure
Their attempts will cease
Those who do not know hate
Will never know love
Those who do not know loss
Will never feel like they've won.

POEM 12
A WINDOW IN
THE BLACK BOX

I lay in a box all black
no colour just blank
As small as my conscience
consumed by my mind's toxins.
Sometimes it's as large as a bay
as hollow as my days.
Although it's a box with a slit
in the walls it's fit
You call it a windowpane
I call it an escape from my pain.

I look out at the view
Same old, nothing new
The freedom of that bird
The people that are like cattle or a herd.
They will follow the wise
Into their own demise
They will follow the powerful
Their own lives sorrowful
They will follow the lover
And forget; don't judge a book by it's cover.
They might even follow you
But you're nothing above their hollow hue.

When I look at this view
Same old, nothing new
I'm reminded of this world's rule
Pick your card, your own fuel
Be the dull leader or disguise like a wise fool.
There are only two routes
Though cattle like you shall remain confused
When I look at you, in this bizarre view
I'm no more crippled by my own routes
I'd rather play the devil with dignity
Than be a pawn in a fool's vicinity.

When I look at this view
Same old, nothing new
I close my eyes and turn away
I'd rather pace in my black box, stare in the hollow bay
Than watch this absurdity unfold day to day.
For one thing I'm reminded of in this world today
Neither of us are as we portray.

When I look at this view
Nothing old, all new
This black box where I now reside
This new person that lives in my mind,
The windowpane to my past's pain
had all to lose, nothing to gain.
I look at the fool that I was back in the day
This new person within me would rather look away.
Yet when I look back, at that bizarre view
I'm no more crippled by my new routes
I'd rather play the devil with dignity
Than be a pawn in a fool's vicinity.

POEM 13
DECIPHER

I'm sad because I'm not happy
I'm happy because I'm not sad
These words I unfortunately fail to understand
They're as hollow as they are bland.

I could give you a smile
Whilst I'm tearing apart inside.
I could shed a tear
Yet hold no fear.
I could wage a war
Yet my heart could remain pure.
My eyes could look as deep as death
You could never guess the depth.

My poems reek of emotions
love, hate, pain and more commotion
But you'll never decipher my mind
To emotions, it is blind.
Although I map all sorts of feelings in my writings
But the real emotion behind it all, is always going to be in hiding.
Although my lines express how much this accursed world hurts,
Yet emotions could never make one like me bend over backwards.

I write about what I hear
What I see
What people fear.
The glee
Masked in despair.
The bird that's free
Yet caged in the air.
Throughout my time there's something that I realised
Love and hate have always been two to be idealised
Yet humans are a race that leave me surprised
Because time after time to these petty emotions, they've
accepted their mind's demise.

My eyes could look as deep as death
You could never guess the depth.
You read these encrypted rhymes to make your heart feel lighter
Think you're not the only one suffering and move to feel wiser,
Of these emotions I ain't no survivor, just a writer
Yet through my poems, my mind could never be deciphered.

POEM 14
DEAR EREN,

You found me when I was alone
In no time I connected with you the most.
I was in a world of hurt
A world of pain
Feelings of despair
Tears of vain
Day and night my eyes would drain.

I watched you all along
Time spent with you never felt too long
You too like me were in a world of pain
a world without hope
a world with no scope
Yet your tears never went in vain.

You kept moving forward by yourself
And watching you I healed myself.

We both saw a world of betrayal
Couldn't give those memories a proper burial.
You too like me, were living in the walls
Only yours were physically concrete
Mine, cemented with deceit.

You taught me how to fight
You made me stronger every night
And all this while, I never realised
At the end of my tunnel, you were the light.
I still watch you everyday
See you struggle in crippling pain
Yet you keep moving forward,
you still have freedom to gain.

But now you're going to leave me
And to visit you I can't find that tree
But a world without you I don't want to see
Just one thing can you promise me?
That you will come in my life again
In my thoughts
In my pain
At my worst
At my gain.

People tell me you still do care
You do love
Even in despair.
Then how come that lesson I couldn't comprehend?
Now there's little time, we're about to reach the end.
I strived so hard to become like you
But now people tell me you're just a story, untrue.
They don't know what it's like for us
Care too much to get wiped away like dust.

But as Fall comes
You will leave me too
Tell me now
How do I move forward without you?
Dear Eren
You found me when I was alone
In no time I connected with you the most.
Now you will leave me just like you found me
But I know you will always be around me
In my thoughts
In my words
In my pain
At my worst .

I will never forget you
In my mind you will be glued
Even if people say you're untrue.
For me, you'll never pass by
In my thoughts I will keep you alive
When you go away, maybe I will cry
But together this world we will survive.
Now in my heart you will reside
And even in the next tunnel, you will be my light.

POEM 15
FROM YOU,
A FEW CHAPTERS AGO

Dear me
If you're reading this
I hope you've found some bliss
I hope you're far away from pain's intense kiss
After all the chances of happiness that you've missed
Now watching you smile is my only wish.

Daily you walk all those miles
Trying to step away from all those lies
Through those painful screeching cries
Anything meaningful, did you realise?
When people ask you about those sad eyes
Do you still say 'I'm fine'?
Knowing you still feel dead inside.

In all other spheres you seem so perfect
Then your own emotions, why do you neglect?
Your work is always on overdrive
Then with your heart, why do you still strive?
Your chest still struggles against that invisible knife
That weapon that vacuums out all your life

The fruit of sadness that you bit into
To which all your hopes suddenly succumbed to.
All those happy times now feel untrue
How much pain is still due for you?
Is this all a blessing in disguise
Then this feeling, why do you despise?

Sometimes it feels unfair
All these emotions , with whom do you share?
No one?
Does that make you feel you've won?
Then why do you pretend your heart is numb?
How far away from your feelings can you run?

Dear me,
If you're reading this
I hope you've found some bliss
All those happy times you thought you missed
When you seemed so lost in that spiralling abyss .
Although dead inside, I know you've come out wise
One day you'll wake up to a beautiful sunrise
With happiness no more will you compromise
That day you'll come to realise
It truly was a blessing in disguise.